THE POWER OF WORDS

The words that I speak to you are spirit and life. John 6:63

James Asante

To order additional copies of this book, contact:
Xlibris Corporation
0-800-644-6988
www.xlibrispublishing.co.uk
Orders@xlibrispublishing.co.uk
301688

Contents

Dedication

This book is dedicated to my Lord and master Jesus Christ by whose grace I have been saved and come this far.

I also dedicate this book to my mother and father who taught our family the fear of the Lord and made many sacrifices for us to have a better life and be a blessing to others.

Acknowledgement

I thank God my sufficiency, who called and chose me to fulfil his purpose by equipping me with grace, wisdom and provision.

I thank "the Asante family" for all their support, unity and love.

I also thank all my pastor-friends and all my church brothers and sisters who have been an immediate family away from home. God bless all the above and others that I could not even mention in this book.

Introduction

I heard a story from a preacher a few years ago which was interesting yet profound and worthy of our deepest thoughts and meditation.

It was a story of a man and wife who sold their house and went all around the world in search of precious gold; only to return to their hometown and find that the land on which their house was located was actually a gold mine.

There are many who do not give attention to what is common. The Bible says in 2 Corinthians 4:7 "but we have this treasure in earthen vessels that the excellency of the power may be of God and not of us".

Most people always want to look to others or outside for needed resources, solution and assistance instead of looking carefully within themselves to discover and make use of the inner resource, solution and strength they have always possessed.

It is not wrong to seek help or pay others to supply needed services. However, understand that there is a hidden potential in you that the world is awaiting its manifestation.

One such common but important potential known to few people are our words.

This book seeks to share some few thoughts in simple terms on this all important potential available to everyone on earth and how to encourage all to be awakened to its usage and benefits.

I believe without a shadow of doubt that you will be blessed and become a blessing as you progress through the pages of this book.

Chapter 1

The Power of Words

Words are spirits

Humans are the highest level of God's creation. He created us in his image and sees himself through us, thus he is able to manifest his full self in and through us. Such manifestations are carried out through our spirits, souls, bodies and words.

It is remarkable that many people do not appreciate, see or realise the importance of words. However a few others recognize the importance, power and impact of words and are able to utilize their words to carry out great feats and bring about changes around them and in this world.

The Lord Jesus said in John 6:63 that *"It is the spirit that gives life. The words that I speak to you are spirit and life".* Also the wise King Solomon said in Proverbs 18:21 that *"Death and life are in the power of the tongue: and they that love it shall eat the fruit thereof".*

We are spirit beings who live in a body and have a soul. Who we are is really the spirit being in us. Our words are spirits because our words come from the spirit within. When we speak we release spirits—"word-spirits". These word-spirits directly come from our spirits.

Our words are droplets and extensions of our spirits. Our words are no different from the character and nature of our spirits. Our words reveal who we truly are. Our words are us.

The word-spirits we release may result in either life or death to us and our hearers hence the need to be mindful and careful of the words we speak and the words we pay attention to.

When we study the life of Jesus, there was no place where Jesus made a statement and said "Oh do not worry about what I just said. I was only joking". No, every word that proceeded out from Jesus' mouth was for a reason and purpose.

Jesus respected and meant every word that proceeded out of His mouth. He was very much aware and understood the impact of the words he released. No wonder he had tremendous results in his earthly ministry.

Jesus spent much time to practically teach His disciples on how to use their words to rule their world. God always touched the spirits of his prophets and kings, and seasoned their tongues before assigning them their prophetic and/or kingly responsibilities.

When the Holy Spirit first descended on the disciples in the upper room, He gave them tongues of fire. (Acts 2).

When we accept the Lordship of Jesus Christ over our lives and become children of God, the Holy Spirit who proceeds from the Father, comes to reside in us, gives us tongues of fire and trains us on how to use our tongues to rule our world for His glory.

> *Our words are spirits and we ourselves are our words.*

He does this by ministering His word to our spirits as we study, meditate on His word and make time to pray in other tongues as He gives us the utterance.

Words are breath and wind

What are words? Words are not just the blue print seen on paper. Words are "breath" or "wind" with meanings released from the person speaking.

Words remain in the atmosphere as spirits. To enable others know the words or breath that went forth in our daily lives, words are recorded on tapes or documented on paper and in books.

Words are breath or wind with interpretational or logical codes for comprehensible and communication purposes. The interpretational codes are the voices that give our words logical sound with meanings that can be interpreted by our brains.

Having said this, we must bear in mind that it is not every logic sound that can be interpreted by our brain. There are some higher logical sounds that can only be interpreted by our spirits.

These logic sounds are spiritual logic sounds. Examples are speaking in other tongues, groaning, wailing, crying and laughing in the spirit.

The meanings of uttered words give value to our words. One word can have different and multiple meanings depending on the context and ease of manipulation of the word. It is therefore imperative to pay close attention to sentences and choices of words people use when they speak.

One can blow wind or air with his mouth. Blowing of air with the mouth or nose (i.e. inhaling or exhaling) is the act of breathing.

However, when logic and audible voices and sounds are added to the inhaled or exhaled air, words results and either our brains or spirits can interpret what was said.

God's breath in creation

Everything we see in creation resulted from God's Word—God's Breath (Genesis 1). After the creation and formation of Adam (man) from the clay of the earth, God breathed the breath of life into man and he became a living being having the same nature as God.

God then gave him responsibility and the ability to rule and be in charge of all that he created.

God gave man a trial of this responsibility and ability by asking him to name the animals (Genesis 2:19). Whatever name man gave to the animals, it became established.

There was no place where man complained of a problem that required God's assistance. When man faced any challenge, all he needed to do was to fix it by speaking forth what he wanted to see. This is dominion and authority.

The problem came about when mankind willingly sold this dominion and authority into the hand of the devil. (Genesis 3).

Glory be to God however that this dominion, authority, and glory was legally taken back by man through the finished work of the Lord Jesus Christ on the cross and his resurrection from the dead.

Mankind need to become aware of what Jesus did, accept it and walk in the light of what has been made available.

We need to understand that every created thing originates from God's breath—His word. Every created thing therefore responds to God's word.

Since man has been given God's kind of nature and ability, all creation also responds to man's words.

Furthermore since the Lord Jesus Christ is the one who redeemed man from his fallen position to a higher authority—this authority being greater than the authority of the first man Adam; God has highly exalted Jesus Christ the Lord and given him a name greater than

> *Decree what you want to see in the name of the Lord Jesus, add the necessary practical actions with patience and an attitude of worship, and see it come to pass.*

every name; that at the mention of the name of Jesus every knee shall bow and every tongue shall confess that Jesus Christ is Lord to the glory of God the Father. (Philippians 2:5-11). Hallelujah!

On the basis of this, man's words and declarations must be affirmed on the name of the Lord Jesus for effectiveness.

Declare what you want to see.

As a result of the righteous act of the Lord Jesus Christ, God has delegated to the name of the Lord Jesus the authority, dominion and privilege of declaring with your mouth what you want to see and actually seeing it happen; such that when you want something done, all you need to do is to decree that thing and affirm it on the name of Jesus. (Job 22:28).

Afterwards add the necessary practical actions to it and you will see it come to pass and established.

The practical operation of the Word of God in this way became evident to me some few years ago:

One day my father and mother planned to visit my grand-mother on my mother's side who lived in Kwahu about three hours' drive from our home in Akosombo, Ghana. They prepared for the journey, got everything ready and at about eight o'clock in the morning set off.

Soon after they left my younger sister Dinah came and told me that my parents forgot to add a container of powdered milk that my grand-mother requested which she really liked.

This item had already been bought however due to the rush of packing and preparing for the journey they forgot to add it to the luggage.

At the time, I had just started learning this operation in the Word of God. So I immediately said a short word of prayer to the Lord for my parents to return. I then commanded under my breath that my parents turn back and come for the container of powdered milk.

In a calm confident voice declared to Dinah that she should take heart because dad and mum will return for the powdered milk.

After about thirty minutes, we heard the honking of my father's car in front of our house. We went out to see them and asked them why they have returned.

They said the car they were travelling with started giving them problems so they thought it wise to return and use our second car for the journey instead. I knew however that it was not just the car giving a problem. I knew it was the Lord who answered my prayer and the effective operation of my words caused things to go in the way I wanted.

I then thanked the Lord and explained it all to Dinah and she also gave praise to the Lord. We added the powdered milk to their luggage as they loaded the stuff onto the second car and they went on their journey.

Praise be to God who hears prayer (Psalm 65:2).

Principle of working the word

I believe that the operation of words works. Ask God what you want by faith. Go ahead and declare or decree what you want to see in the name of the Lord Jesus, add the necessary actions with patience and you will see it come to pass.

Words minister to our spirits.
They impact and build our souls and bodies

Proverbs 16:24 says *"Pleasant words are as an honey comb, sweet to the soul and health to the bones"* and Proverbs 27:17 says *"Iron sharpens iron so a man sharpens the countenance of his friend"*

The wise king Solomon said pleasant words are sweet to the soul and health to our bones.

The Bible compares our spirits and words to an iron. In the same way that iron is sharpened with another iron, the words of friends sharpen and condition our spirits when we give attention to what these friends tell us.

For example when you are downhearted and discouraged and a friend gives you a word of encouragement or you hear good news, you immediately become revived and refreshed.

Once the word enters your spirit, you receive a new urge and strength to go on and not to give up. In the same way a hurtful and bitter word released from a person, aimed directly at you or someone you love can break you down, wound your spirit and even cause you to have a bad day.

It therefore implies that the information and words we pay attention to over a short or prolonged period of time go a long way to influence, shape and build our character, spirit, soul and body.

Many people underestimate the power of the words they speak over themselves and words they attend to. They think words are "nothing"—not important.

They think the purpose of words is to just communicate, convey information and interact. Others do not give consideration to the importance of words although they spend years going to school to study to become professionals in different areas of specialism.

Some forget that it was the words they read and attended to in their different areas of study that made them who they are. After series of examinations they proved by excellent grades that they were conversant in the words they were taught in school and were awarded certificates and degrees in their fields of study.

We are made by words. Jesus said in Mark 1:17 "...follow me and I will make you to become..." Jesus was not just asking his disciples to follow him wherever he went but to follow him in his word. Jesus' words revealed His nature, character, life and glory (which are also God's nature, character, life and glory).

By following and giving attention to Jesus' words you become transformed into that same nature, character, life and glory. The song below written by Tom M. Jones emphasizes this point:

Song:

Let the beauty of Jesus be seen in me,
All His tender compassion and purity,
Oh Thou Spirit divine,
On my nature refine,
Till the beauty of Jesus, is seen in me.

As we follow and give attention to the Word of God, we are actually allowing our nature to be refined by the divine Spirit of God and the result of this will be the beauty of Jesus revealed in our lives.

The primary requirement

I remember asking my friends at work what they thought God primarily required of them. They were very interested in that question and gave me series of answers.

Among these answers were: God requires us to give offerings, God requires us to help others and give alms, and God wants us to win people for Jesus.

Though all their answers were okay, the Spirit of God gave me what I believe was the first and foremost requirement of God. **It is our attention to His word.**

When I said this, my friends were surprised and quite disappointed. Why? This is because they underestimated the power of words. I believe we will receive the same kind of response and reaction from most people, were we to put this same question to them.

Our attention to God's word is the first step that brings us into the glory life of God and makes us partakers and sharers of God's divine nature.

The Bible says that God's hidden secret which the world cannot receive is "Christ in you, the hope of Glory". (Colossians 2:26-27; 1 Corinthians 2:7). The bible refers to Christ in 1 John 1:1 as the word of life and the living word.

> *Continuous and consistent attention to words brings transformation.*

To have "the hope of glory" is not only to anticipate a future glorious life but also to live, dwell and walk in glory in every area of your life daily.

"Christ in me; the hope of glory" can therefore be paraphrased and read as: "the living word of God in me continually (i.e. Christ in me), causes me to live the life of glory (i.e. the hope of glory).

The life of glory is a life above sin, sickness, failure, disease, death, etc. This is God's mystery unveiled to humankind. As we listen to God's word, we receive God's breath into our spirits. We are thereby imparted with God's life and anything contrary to God such as sickness, sin, failure, disease, death, etc., automatically departs.

This is the reason why it is imperative to give adequate and quality time to listen, study and meditate on the Word of God.

It is also one of the main reasons why the Spirit of God admonishes us in Hebrews 10:25 to be consistent in our church attendance.

This is because our continual church attendance gives us the opportunity to hear the Word of God consistently. And the continual and consistent attention to the Word of God will result in our healing (equipping, empowering, strengthening, helping, correcting etc.) as revealed in Psalm 107:20—*"He (God) sent his Word and healed them, and delivered them from their destructions."*

Jesus also said in John 8:32 *"And you will know the truth, and the truth will make you free."*

A one-off attention to the Word of God may not bring healing but a continual exposure to the Word of God will surely bring and establish healing and health in your life.

If you will go to church consistently, pay attention to
believe the Word, Submit yourself to the leadings of the
and get involved in church worship and service, I can as
that there is no situation that will be impossible to change.

> **Consistent and continual attention and exposure to the Word of God produces automatic healing**

It is not enough to go to
to hear the Word of God. You
to get anointed messages, make
to listen to them consistently
read other Christian literature wh
taking time out to meditate on th
Word of God continually.

It is healing and salvation to dwell and remain under the sound
of the Word of God.

Having said this, it must be noted that the Holy Spirit may
want you to either preach, teach or listen to a particular message
repeatedly over a period of time.

If the Holy Spirit requires this of you, there's no reason to argue
with him or get bored. As the head of the Church, the Holy Spirit
may want to do a good work in or through you, for which reason he
requires you to be equipped with the material of his word, otherwise
that good work may not come to pass. This is because the Lord does
not do anything outside his Word.

> John 1:3 says "All things were made by him; and without
> him was not anything made that was made."

lso consistent attention to the same message repeatedly
the message to be ingrained in our spirits, souls and bodies
g the message in and through our lives.

This reveals God's graciousness and goodness. God wants his ids to dwell and walk in divine healing and health. He therefore gives us the material to make this possible—**His Word.**

He sends us his Word and heals our diseases and he further admonishes us to go to church continually, where we can hear his Word consistently to remain healthy and take his divine healing to the world.

Praise the Lord!

The Bible says in Psalm 107:20 that *"He sent His word and healed them and delivered them from their destructions".*

When we spend time daily feeding on the word and listening to anointed messages, we are automatically cleansed from sin, sin consciousness (the thought or feeling that one has sinned meanwhile he has not sinned), sicknesses and diseases.

Jesus said in John 15:3 *"... You are clean through the word I have spoken unto you."*

The Word of God is what cleanses you from sin, infirmity and disease. The Word of God directly mends the sicken state of your spirit to produce healing in the physical body. The Word of God also renews and strengthens you.

When you are studying a particular anointed message c
the bible, do not be in a hurry to go on to the next mes′
Consistent attention to the same message and boo′
cause the message and words to be engrained ⁚
will become that message and word.

When the message enters your spi.
and the word and speak it out aloud to you.
You will eventually become what you say.

If you require that word or message to affect something or someone, direct the words or message to that thing or person and voice it out aloud in Jesus name continually and you will see the person or thing eventually becoming what you said or influenced by it.

The whole of Psalm 29 talks about what the voice of the Lord does once it is voiced through us.

It says in verse 5 that *"the voice of the Lord breaks the cedars of Lebanon" (ESV).* This means that the word of the Lord that you give voice to can destroy any difficult situation you are facing in your life right now.

It also says in verse 9 that *"the voice of the Lord makes the deer give birth" (ESV).* In order words the word of the Lord that you give voice to can give you the enablement to give birth whether you are barren or have problem of giving birth.

When doing the above, do not doubt and start asking yourself questions such as: "How will it happen?" In the same way you do not worry about how the force of gravity will bring you back to the ground when you jump up; do not worry about how it is going to happen.

The operation of the force of gravity is a law and it does not fail when all the conditions are adhered to. In a similar manner the operation of feeding our spirits with God's words and using our mouths to declare what we want to see based on God's words and seeing it come to pass is also a law—the law of faith.

This law does not fail provided all the conditions are satisfied. Romans 3:27 confirms that faith is a law. Like all other laws, it will not fail when all the required conditions are satisfied.

Conditions of the law of faith

Some examples of conditions that must be satisfied for the law of gravity to function on a body is that the body must be on earth and the body must have mass etc.

Conditions that must be satisfied for the law of faith to work is as follows:

- First, you must hear the word of God (Romans 10:17); i.e. you must give attention to God's word.

- Second, boldly speak what you want to see based on God's word in Jesus name (Matthew 21:21).

- Third, believe and do not doubt that what you said will come to pass (Mark 11:22-23).

- Fourth, give thanks and glory to God continually for the manifestation of what you declared. (1 Thessalonians 5:18).

- Fifth, add the necessary practical actions (James 2:26).

- Sixth, make it a habit to give quality time of heart felt worship to the Lord (Psalm 149:1-8).

The bible says in Isaiah 50:10 that *"Who is among you that fears the Lord, that obeys the voice of his servant, that walks in darkness, and hath no light? Let him trust in the name of the Lord and stay upon his God".*

To stay upon the Lord is to hold onto the Word of the Lord (through your belief and confession of the word) and to worship him by singing songs of worship and pouring words of adoration to the Lord as you allow your spirit to minister to God.

Practicing the law and operations of faith makes you better at it.

When you do this, the Lord promises in Psalm 149:4 that he will beautify you with salvation.

You need to understand that God knows what you are passing through and your need of salvation. In fact in Christ he has completed the work of salvation and when you practice the above and worship the Lord, your expectation will be made manifest in the physical.

In the same way that we all had to learn and practise walking when we were little, there is the need for us to learn and practise the above operation with patience as children of God until we get better at it.

This brings back memory on an event that happened a few years back when I was in secondary school.

On this occasion we were taking our mock examination for the senior secondary school certificate exam. We were told before the start of the exams that we must ensure we owed no school fees.

All pupils owing school fees will not be allowed to take the exams and they will be ushered out of the exams hall (—a very embarrassing scene).

I knew my siblings and I owed an enormous amount of fees because my father used to give me the money to pay our school fees at the start of every term.

I told God to have mercy on me, see me through the exams and provide us with money to settle the school fees. I trusted the Lord and went in to the exam hall to take the exams.

Mid-way through the exam, the assistant head master of the school, came with a few other teachers; stood in front and started mentioning the names of the pupils who owed. All the students whose names were mentioned had to leave the hall immediately.

Amazingly my name was not mentioned. I was very surprised and I thanked God under my breath that my name was not mentioned. I did not know and cannot explain why my name was not mentioned although I owed.

I believed however that it was God who worked it out such that my name was not mentioned. I then said that as he had orchestrated events in this way, I believe he is able, and will clear all our school fees for us. I continued by saying that how he will do it I did not know but I leave it with him and I thank him in advance for paying all our fees for us.

I finished the exams and went home praising God and still musing over the miracle that I was not dismissed from the exams hall.

Later in the afternoon of the same day, my sister Dinah came home rejoicing and all excited. We asked her what was exciting her.

She then said that one of the Japanese teachers—Mr Utakah who had come to our school on a teaching volunteer program asked her about our school fees in a conversation and has decided to pay all our school fees for us.

I was astonished beyond measure and continued to say: Glory to God, Jesus is Lord . . . We broke the news to our parents and the whole family. They were very surprised and very grateful and thankful to

God for his extraordinary favour. We then went to see the Japanese teacher that same evening to thank him for his kind gester.

I knew however that it was God who orchestrated all these events. Glory be to his holy name!

Words produce glory

> *We become changed into God's glory by listening to his word.*

God is a good and merciful God. He has made it possible and accessible for us all to partake and share in his glory. God is His Word, and the Word of God is God (John 1:1).

When we pay attention to His word, we become transformed into his Word. 1 Corinthians 2:7 says *"But we speak the wisdom of God (i.e. the Word of God) in a mystery, even the hidden wisdom, which God ordained before the world unto our glory".*

After man sinned and fell short of God's glory, God solved the problem and brought man back again to glory through the agency of his Word which is the wisdom of God. We become changed into God's glory when we attend to His Word by paying attention to the Word and doing the Word.

to an

Gabriel
d those
ception

a child is
l parent.
e his child
ing words

responding
ords and as
spirit of the
word/spirit

any problem
adopted child
the child is his

cteristics of his
irit, personality,

ossible. Through
word-children as
carry our nature,
ation.
cal parent that has

Chapter 2

ren and Word children

ove discussions that God created all
made by words, that we can make
ords, and that our words are us.

sometimes meet people of other
news of Christ.

th everything but the part they
Jesus Christ is the son of God
n we believe in Him.

d many sincere people from
and becoming children of
ovisions and privileges of
he world to come.

ade in two ways. Most
f making children but
n.

erms into the womb
. This is the way in

In the word-way, seed-words are also implanted i individual to form a new person out of the old person.

An example of this is found in the life of Jesus where angel came to impart words into Mary and when Mary accepte anointed and blessed words, the words resulted in the co of baby Jesus. (Luke 1:26-38).

Another example of the word-way is observed when adopted by someone who was not originally the biologica

The adopted parent can transform the child to becom or mould the child into the person he wants by impar into the adopted child over a period of time.

For the transformation to be effective; love, co actions and prayers must be added to the imparted w this parent patiently and purposefully nurtures the child with gracious words, the desired child results—a **child**.

An adoptive parent in this way does not have or hesitance of transferring all of his wealth to his because although the child is not his biological child true child.

The adopted child may bear the physical chara biological parents but he actually carries the sp character and nature of the adoptive parents.

The impartation of word-spirits made this p this process therefore we can make as many possible during our life-time on earth who will spirit, character and personality into their gener

We need to realize that, it is not the biologi the upper hand but the adoptive parent.

[This world has seen different ages in history. There was the industrial age in the 19th and 20th centuries. We are now in the information age where ones possession, wielding and control of quality information result in power, influence and wealth. I believe we are entering another age where power, influence and wealth will not only be measured by how industrious you are or how much quality information you control, but how many word-children you possess.]

I started observing this phenomenon in my own way when my mother adopted a child from a distant relative in our village whose father passed away when the child was born.

The boy's name was Kwame and my mother and father named him Enoch Asante but I nick-named him Mr-Kwame-boy. He was three years old at the time of adoption and his mother gladly gave her full consent for my mother to adopt her son.

When my mother brought Enoch home, she and my father treated and looked after him in the same way they did us.

At the time, I had to stay at home for about eight months waiting for my junior secondary school certificate examination results before I went to the senior secondary school. Because of this I spent more time during the day baby-sitting Enoch.

As time went on, Mr-Kwame-boy became more close to me and related with me better than anyone else. (I was about fifteen years of age at this time).

During this period, Kwame could only speak the local language—Akan, but not a word in English.

I always loved to have my personal worship time with the Lord where I poured my heart to the Lord, worshipped him, prayed for others and studied the bible.

One day when I was praying, I asked God to help me to speak English fluently because I realised my English was not very good and I was not very confident when communicating in the language.

The Lord drew my attention to Mr-Kwame-boy and asked me to start teaching and speaking only English with him. God told me that in time Mr-Kwame-boy will begin to speak in English and at the same time my English will improve and I will be confident in expressing myself.

The idea sounded good. I thanked the Lord and started teaching and speaking only English with him. Some relatives ridiculed me a bit but I was not discouraged.

After some time all the ridicules ceased and I noticed Mr-Kwame-boy speaking English with me. My family realised it as well and they were very impressed.

To me however it was a miracle I will never forget. Praise be to God!

> **Your true children are those that were made by your words.**

After a few months, Mr-Kwame-boy was rattling in English and amazingly I noticed improvement in my English. I decided therefore to speak only English when I go to the university.

About two years into university, my English had improved to the extent that a room-mate asked me once if I actually spoke our local language at all.

I laughed and responded in the affirmative. The Lord is good and he practically answers our prayers.

A parent is not necessarily one who has given birth biologically to a child but one who has imparted his or her nature and spirit into that child through words.

God's intention is to make us his sons—sons through words. God's son is his Word. His intention therefore is to make us his word—his sons.

This is the way in which God gave birth to us Christians and is still giving birth to countless number of Christians all around the world.

We become sons and daughters of God first of all by using our mouths to confess the Lordship of the Lord Jesus Christ over our lives and believing with our hearts that God raised Him from the dead.

Once we do this, we affirm that we are not our own or the devil's property but God's property; and that we have chosen to believe, accept and conform to every word of God without doubt.

By this act, God's life and nature is imparted into our spirits making us sons of God.

Romans 10:9-10 says "That if you shall confess with your mouth the Lord Jesus and shall believe in your heart that God raised him from the dead, you shall be saved. For with the heart man believes unto righteousness, and with the mouth confession is made unto salvation."

This scripture makes us to know that, after believing with our hearts, we must confess with our mouths in order to complete the work of salvation.

This is the way through which we become children of God. It is also the way through which we order our lives as Christians and are able to receive anything from God and make things happen:

We believe with our hearts what we want to see in accordance with God's word; we confess with our mouth what we want to see and we see that thing done.

Word-Children grow by the word

Every natural and normal child is expected to grow. Children grow by feeding on breast-milk and other suitable foods after they are weaned to enable them grow healthily.

Children born by the word of God must also grow and continue to grow until they become mature word-children in all areas—in wisdom, stature, knowledge and understanding and ultimately to be as Christ in all his fullness. We can do this by feeding and dwelling in the word of God i.e. studying and meditating on the bible for ourselves and supplementing it with other anointed Christian teaching tapes and literature.

In Acts 20:32 we read of Apostle Paul's prayer to God for the Ephesian church just before leaving them—*"And now brethren, I commend you to God and to the word of his grace which is able to build you up and to give you an inheritance among all them which are sanctified".*

> *Continuous attention to the word of God will transform you into God's glory.*

The Word of God is that which builds us up and empowers us to get our inheritance on earth—nothing else does.

When we study the Word and meditate on the Word we eventually become the Word and we radiate the glory of the Word.

2 Corinthians 3:18 says *"But we all, with open face beholding as in a glass the glory of the Lord, are changed into the same image from glory to glory even as by the Spirit of the Lord."*

Continuous attention to the word will transform us into God's glory. So do not be tired to allow a day to pass without giving attention to the word of God.

Chapter 3

The Word quickens our mortal bodies

There is a powerful and interesting piece of scripture that I love to meditate on time and again.

I believe it will further throw more light on what we have been discussing and help encourage us as word-sons and word-daughters to know the Word of God, fill our spirits with the Word of God and walk by the Word of God.

Romans 8:11 says *"But if the spirit of him that raised up Jesus from the dead dwell in you, he that raised up Christ from the dead shall also quicken your mortal bodies by his spirit that dwells in you".*

Also Romans 6:4 says *". . . Christ was raised up from the dead by the glory of the Father . . ."* 1 Peter 4:14 and 2 Corinthians 3:18 make reference to the Holy Spirit as the Spirit of Glory.

If the Holy Spirit is the glory of God and Christ was raised from the dead by the glory of the Father, it implies that Christ was actually raised from the dead by the Holy Spirit. Hallelujah!

The good news is that the glorious Holy Spirit came to reside in our hearts when we confessed the Lordship of Christ Jesus over our lives.

The word then continues to tell us in Romans 8:11 that "if the spirit of him that raised up Jesus from the dead dwell in you, he that raised up Christ from the dead shall also quicken your mortal bodies by his spirit that dwells in you.

We have known from the previous chapters however that "spirit" can mean breath or word, we therefore can paraphrase Romans 8:11 and read it in this way:

*"If the **word** of the **Holy Spirit** who raised up Jesus from the dead dwell in you, the **Holy Spirit** that raised up Christ from the dead shall also quicken (or give life, health, peace, divine ability, strength, etc. to) your mortal bodies by his **word** that dwells in you.*

The understanding of the word of God in this way, makes us to know that once we open our spirits to the word of God by giving attention to the anointed word of God and doing the word, (i.e. confessing the word with our mouth and backing it with corresponding actions) we will have no choice but walk in divine health, life and unexplainable peace. Hallelujah!

The good news is that we have easy access to the word of God. The glorious word of God (the bible and anointed messages from preachers all over the world) is in our reach. Hallelujah!

Let us therefore endeavour to fill our hearts and minds with the word of God by studying and meditating on the words in the bible and confessing or prophesying the words we want to see in our life and in our world.

Do not speak what you are seeing. Speak forth what you want to see and you will see it come to pass and the negative situation you are facing will change.

Consistent and continual confession of the word of God is what guarantees materialisation of the word. In Genesis 3:15, God prophesied the coming of the Christ to solve man's problem of sin.

Many of the prophets of old thereafter maintained the confessions about the coming of the Christ or the Messiah and his life and assignment on earth.

In the fullness of time, Christ the Lord came to earth to fulfil the assignment of bringing man back to glory—the glory of God!

John 1:14 says *"And the Word was made flesh and dwelt among us and we beheld his glory, the glory as in the only begotten of the Father..."*

The Word will surely materialise; it will definitely become flesh if word-children of God do not give up their confessions of the Word of God.

As a child of God, be determined and do not give in to problems, sin, sickness, disease, poverty or death. Confess the word un-dauntingly based on your understanding of the Word of God and it will by all means come to pass.

Hebrews 4:12-13 says *"For the word of God is quick (i.e. living) and powerful, and sharper than any two-edged sword, piercing even to the dividing asunder of the soul and spirit, and of the joints and marrow, and is a discerner of the thoughts and intents of the heart.*

Neither is there any creature that is not manifest in his sight: but all things are naked and opened unto the eyes of him with whom we have to do".

This piece of scripture is very powerful. The writer says that the Word of God is living, the word is powerful, piercing, a discerner, and the word sees all things.

> *We are made by words. Our words directly affect our physical bodies.*

The writer again personalises the word and says that all things are manifest in **his** sight. This is who we become when we dwell on the word and give attention to it.

In fact we become extraordinary and super human; because the word translates us from humans to gods. Yes sons and daughters of God. (Psalm 82:6).

Let's therefore take our place as sons and daughters of God and speak forth the Word that we truly are and live it out. Praise the Lord forevermore!

Chapter 4

Other Tongues—Tongues of fire

Acts 2:1-4 gives a vivid, remarkable and beautiful description of what happened on the day of Pentecost.

When the Holy Spirit made his entrance and residence in the hearts of men, there appeared cloven tongues of fire on their heads and they were filled with the Spirit and all of them began to speak in other tongues as the Spirit gave them utterance.

The appearance of the cloven tongues of fire on their heads was a symbolic truth of what happens when Christians speak with other tongues.

"Other-tongues" are words of fire released into the spirit realm. The words of fire know how to deal with the problem at hand when they are released.

Such tongues released at the time of worship as led by the Spirit, will also be the right words of worship required for the Lord.

I dreamt sometime ago and I saw myself praying in other tongues. As I continued praying, fire was released and started burning around a house I knew. I then saw snakes coming out of that house and fleeing.

When I intensified praying in other tongues, the intensity of the fire increased and when I reduced the intensity of my praying the fire reduced in intensity.

Afterwards I woke up and pondered the dream over and over again.

I realised that praying in other tongues is actually releasing fire in the realms of the spirit to destroy the works of the Devil and establish the kingdom of God.

There are untold benefits to the believer as he or she spends purposeful time to pray in tongues and worship the Lord.

After studying and meditating on the word we need to spend time praying in the Spirit. By this our spirits receive extraordinary enlightenment and understanding into the Word of God that will be hidden to the ordinary man or the Christian who does not pray in tongues.

When you pray in tongues not only is your spiritual eyes opened to discern hidden things of the Word of God and of life in general, you also receive divine ability, grace, inner strength and the propelling force to put into practice or act on what you have discovered in the Word of God and received into your spirit.

This special insight, knowledge, ability and wisdom gives you the leverage and advantage over other people and even other Christians who do not pray in other tongues or underestimate the power of praying in tongues.

Tongues of Angels

Other-tongue is a heavenly language. It is the language of the angels of God. (1 Corinthians 13:1).

Other-tongue is a special gift and ability given by God to us his saints who have confessed the Lordship of Jesus Christ over our lives.

We may not understand other-tongues with our minds or intellects (1 Corinthians 14:2); however we can receive or pick up the understanding or interpretation in our spirits when we are led by the Spirit of God to utter prophetic-tongues.

To utter Prophetic-tongues is to speak in other tongues with interpretation in explicable words such as prophecies under the unction or inspiration of the Holy Spirit.

I had a dream on another occasion and saw myself talking with two angels in other tongues.

In the conversation my spirit seemed to understand perfectly what they were saying and I responded back to their satisfaction while they also talked backed.

My intellect however could not understand any of the discussion. Afterward they went away.

This dream confirmed what Apostle Paul said in 1 Corinthians 13:1 that other-tongue is an angelic language.

When we speak in other tongues based on our understanding of the word of God, our spirits are renewed and this renewing affects our soul and eventually appears on our bodies.

Our bodies then reflect the glory of God and every other aspect of our lives receives the glory also.

The key ingredient

All the above of course must be founded on love—the love of God in our hearts. That is why it is imperative for Christians to pray in other-tongues based on their knowledge of the Word of God.

This is because, when the Word of God saturates your heart, the result will undoubtedly be his love in your heart flowing to reach and touch others.

By this, your prayer will not be self-centred and selfish but God-centred and others-centred. Also your needs will be met without a care from you.

I will encourage Christians who have confessed the Lordship of Jesus over their lives and have been baptized in the Holy Spirit and speak in other tongues to intensify and increase their prayers in other tongues based on knowledge of the Word of God.

For Christians who do not speak in other tongues but truly desire the infilling of the Spirit of God and grace to speak in other-tongues, I will lead you in prayer to receive the baptism or infilling of the spirit to speak in other-tongues.

Notice that, you receive the baptism of the spirit after you believe and confess the Lordship of Christ over your life.

We will base our prayer on Romans 10:9-10. Can you sincerely open your heart to God and pray this prayer out loud after me:

Prayer:

Father God, I confess with my mouth that Jesus is Lord over my life and everything.

I believe in my heart that You raised him from the dead.

Lord Jesus, infill and baptise me with the Holy Spirit and fire; and with the evidence of speaking in other tongues.

Thank you Father in the name of the Lord Jesus.

Amen.

After this prayer, know that you have been born-again, baptised and filled with the Holy Spirit. Begin then to thank God audibly for his grace and gift and answered prayer.

As you keep thanking and adoring God you will sense an urge to release these "strange" words (other tongues or spiritual language) you have never spoken before bubbling within your spirit.

Take a step of faith and open your mouth now and release and utter the new tongues and words that are bubbling on the inside of you and praise the Lord with the new words.

> *Words are fire in the spiritual realm.*

Do not try to reason them with your brains. Continue speaking in this new language of other tongues and the Spirit of God will add more vocabulary to it for you.

Also your vocabulary in other tongues expands as you study the word of God, listen to anointed messages, meditate on the Word of God and wait on the Lord.

During these quality times with the Lord you will realise that deep and spontaneous tongues will just well up within your spirit. And you cannot but open your mouth and release these tongues to God's glory.

Sometimes they may come in the form of prophetic tongues of which the Spirit of God will give you the interpretation.

The key to effective words

By your continual speaking in tongues, studying and meditating on the Word of God, your boldness in the Lord will increase and your ability to conceptualize and understand spiritual things will broaden.

Your spirit will then send the right logical words to your mind for your mouth to utter and prophecy in every situation and you will see the manifestation of these words and prophecies in the physical.

Your words will become effective and none of them will fall to the ground. Your words will go and fulfil the purpose for which you send them.

Another way of making your words effective is ensuring that you bind yourself to your words at all times even when joking.

By this I mean you must mean every word that proceeds out of your mouth. For example when you jokingly tell kids that you will get them sweets if they stop being naughty, you must ensure that you keep to your word.

When you keep to your words in simple matters, your words will be effective and "keep" to you; and all creation, people and systems both physical and spiritual will respect and respond to your words.

You also need to realise that the quality of your words are determined by the information you have inside your spirit.

Jesus said in Luke 6:45 that "A good man out of the good treasure of his heart brings forth that which is good; and an evil man out of the evil treasure of his heart brings forth that which is evil: for out of the abundance of the heart his mouth speaks".

As human beings we feed our spirit through what we hear, see and pay attention to.

If we pay attention to God's word we will build up our spirits (Acts 20:32), and bring forth quality and effective words that will affect others and us positively.

If we pay attention to useless things which do not matter we will be filling our spirits with junk resulting in worthless and ineffective words that will not give grace to our hearers or we ourselves.

Keying into the realm of the spirit

Whatever we see in the physical is controlled by the spiritual.

I have had the experience of having a dream and seeing that event come to pass in the physical few days after I had the dream.

Many people think that once they see something in their dreams or in the realm of the spirit they cannot do anything about it.

No, God reveals things to us in order to direct or redeem us.

Our words are the instruments we utilise to key into the realm of the spirit to control events, take charge of situations and make effective changes that will manifest in the physical.

When you go out to work or meet people in the streets and you engage them in a conversation, you will immediately discover the negativity in their speech.

Most of these negative words are based on what they are facing, how tough and difficult the economy is, the uncertainty of their future, the bad report the doctor gave them concerning their health and the like.

They may want to talk the same negativity into you, however recognise that you are not of this world if you are a child of God.

If you have confessed the Lordship of Christ over your life, you are not of this world. You are in the world to represent God therefore that evil report does not and must not affect you.

When someone talks negative to you, tell yourself or tell the person that you refuse those words in your life in the name of the Lord Jesus.

Even if you are experiencing negative things in your life, set your gaze on the Word of God and tell yourself: *"It is well with me"* (Isaiah 3:10; Psalm 128:2; Ecclesiastes 8:12). *"All things are working together for my good"* (Romans 8:28). *"I will not die but live to declare the works of the Lord in the name of the Lord Jesus"*. (Psalm118:17). Glory to God!

Do not say it once or twice and stop. Continue to say it until it becomes a part of you and you will see it manifesting in your life.

Understand that your mouth was not given to you to complain about your situation, what is happening or what you are going through.

As a child of God, your mouth is a powerful weapon given to you by God to declare what you want to see; and what you declare will come to pass. It must be noted that you become better at it through continuous practice.

Good life begins with words

Healing for your physical body begins with what you say. It does not start with the medicine you take but the words you speak.

If you say to yourself that *"with the stripes of Jesus I was healed"*—1 Peter 2:24 and that you refuse to be sick, the sickness on your physical body will not stay but die and leave your body.

Words become laws when they proceed out of our mouths. The healing of our physical bodies and our prosperity begins with our words.

Set your gaze on Jesus and what he did on the cross for you; you will definitely recover quicker than you anticipated.

Also your prosperity is preceded by your words. Engage in conversation with wealthy people and you will discover the quality of their words and the positivity in their confessions and communication.

Even when they make losses or things do not go according to their plan they maintain a positive confession and attitude. With time, they gain new ideas that will make way for new fortunes.

Every good thing required in life begins with words. This way of life is seen in the lives of all the people who walked with God in the bible.

Chapter 5

Words are Instructions and we are words

Words are instructions issued for purposes and assignments. The Bible says in Isaiah 9:8 that *"The Lord sent a word into Jacob, and it has lighted upon Israel"*

Isaiah 55:11 says that the word that God has released *"will not return to him void but it will fulfil the purpose for which it was sent by God and it shall prosper in the thing for which God sent it"*.

God sent his Word, Jesus Christ, to fulfil an eternal assignment on earth.

Everything Jesus did was already written in the laws and prophets. Hebrews 10:7 says *"... in the volume of the book it is written concerning me (Jesus Christ) to do your will, O God."*

Jesus knew what his assignment was. He maintained his focus and carried out the instruction God gave him to the letter.

We spirit-children born of the Word of God need to realise that we are God's *individual word* on earth.

We carry specific assignments and special instruction to fulfil God's good will on earth.

The instructions become clear when we become born-again. The Holy Spirit drops the assignment into our hearts and clarifies it as we journey with him in the Word of God—the bible.

When we practically begin to carry out the assignment, the Lord makes available every provision, resource, people, grace, ability, wisdom, understanding and insight required to fulfil the assignment.

When you get to a stage while undertaking your assignment and you think you require anything, first discuss it with God and speak into being what you want to see in Jesus' name.

God will ensure that angels are dispatched on your behalf to assist you in fulfilling this wonderful assignment.

Your Assignment

The vital question you as a Christian must ask is: What is my assignment? Am I fulfilling it or wasting precious time? What has been written of me in the volume of the word of God? Who am I? What word am I?

If you are not confident in answering the above questions, say a short word of prayer now to the Father and ask him to reveal to you your purpose or assignment in life; afterwards go to the bible with sincere heart and open to the place the Lord leads.

He will surely make known to you the-assignment for which he created you.

You are too special and your life is too precious to be wasted or lived unfulfilled.

True excitement, satisfaction and fulfilment in life are found when you discover your assignment in life and live to fulfil it.

It may not be easy to carry it out but with determination, focus, the help of the Holy Spirit, the Word of God and the ministry of angels of God, you will be successful.

You must realise that this is what your life is about and no one in this whole world can do it apart from you.

God the Father, the Lord Jesus, Holy Spirit, heavenly angels and precious people whose life depend on the fulfilment of your assignment are all counting on you.

You cannot afford to fail, become discouraged or give up on the precious assignment for which God created you.

Isaiah 42:4 Says "... *You shall not fail or be discouraged until you have set judgement in the earth; and the isles will wait for your law*".

God needs you, the world needs you and I need you. Therefore be strengthened and encouraged and go on with renewed vigour to fulfil the special purpose for which you were born and complete the key assignment for which you are on earth.

The Lord shall be your strength, shield and buckler. Fear not. You can do it!

For some people, they have known their purpose and assignment but they wonder how they will ever get it done since it is so big a task.

Such people must first recognise that God never gives anyone a task that is less than their strength.

God always gives his children tasks greater than themselves to require his involvement in its accomplishment.

Moreover we need to understand that for every assignment that God gives there is a resultant element or by-product of glory in its fulfilment that must go to God.

For this reason, God always becomes interested in assisting us to successfully accomplish the assignment.

When the assignment is successfully and gloriously accomplished he will receive the glory.

Also we need to understand that the "how" of undertaking the assignment is in the instruction that God gives concerning our assignment in life.

So prayerfully re-visit and meditate on the instruction of the assignment over and over again as you strategize to fulfil it and always submit the revised strategy to Holy Spirit for scrutiny, comments and/or approval.

Life is really sweet and fulfilling when you discover and live to accomplish your purpose. Praise the Lord!

A name is a word

In the kingdom of God and in the realm of the spirit names are very important.

True excitement, satisfaction and fulfilment in life are found when you discover your assignment in life and you live to fulfil it.

The name of a person is a word which defines a person's life, address, purpose and destiny in life.

When we study the bible we realise that God either changed or gave new names to all the people he walked with.

Abram's name was changed to Abraham; Sarai to Sarah, Jacob to Israel etc. The men and women whose names were changed lived new lives consistent with their new names.

What is your name? I am not talking about the name in your passport or on your national identity card but rather the name by which you are called of God.

Once you know and recognise this name your identity and life assignment will be clarified and every resource will be made available to enable you to fulfil the responsibility assigned you by God.

Conclusion

We need to understand that the responsibility is in our hands. As God's children, God has delegated all his authority and power to us in Christ.

If we do not say and do anything, nothing will happen.

I believe all of us Christians need to take the doing part of God's word more serious in order to see the living Word of God manifested in our lives.

Incidentally, part of the "doing" aspect of God's word is our personalisation and confession of the Word of God until we see the Word become manifested in our lives.

Psalm 23:1 says *"the Lord is my shepherd I shall not want . . ."* If even things are not moving on as we expect in our finances we need to continue to declare with our mouths and believe in our hearts that in accordance with Psalm 23:1, we shall not want; and open our spirits to receive divine ideas from the Lord.

In time, extraordinary doors will be opened and we will see monies coming in.

1 Peter 2:24 says *" . . . with the stripes of Jesus we have been healed . . ."* A Christian who needs healing for his physical body must

personalise this word and declare that "I refuse to be sick because with the stripes of Jesus I was healed . . ."

Christians need to be bold and not give in to sickness, sin, poverty nor give up to failure.

And it starts with the confessions of our mouths based on the Word of God and corresponding actions.

Psalm 8:2 says *"In the mouth of babes and sucklings has God ordained strength because of the enemies . . . that the enemy will be silenced . . ."*

Also, Hebrews 13:5-6 says *". . . for God has said . . . so we (Christians) may boldly say: the Lord is my helper . . ."*

The purpose of God's Word is for us to say and live in accordance with what God said.

The Word of God is powerful but if Christians don't put the Word in their hearts and voice it out consistently and continually (and of course add corresponding actions), things will not shift.

Many Christians are praying and waiting on God to do something however God is rather waiting on Christians to speak the Word and the Holy Spirit and angels of God will ensure that the word materialises.

When Jesus was on earth, He used His words to control situations. He spoke what he wanted to see.

When he was leaving, he delegated that responsibility to us who believe in him by asking his Holy Spirit to dwell in us.

This is what makes us victors and overcomers in this world.

This is something more than gold—The Holy Spirit in us, the word of God in our hearts, and the confessions of the Word of God with our mouths; and confirms what a Pentecostal song writer once wrote:

"Something more than Gold,
something more than gold.
The Spirit of God in the heart of man
is something more than Gold"

The responsibility is in our hands. As God's children, God has delegated all his authority and power to us in Christ.

If we do not say or do anything, nothing will happen.

I truly believe that the above thoughts has encouraged and inspired a new urge in you to fill your heart with God's Word and rule your world with your word.

God bless you!

References

All references were taken from King James Version (KJV) and The English Standard Version (ESV) of the bible.